ENJOYING THE GOSPEL

By Eric William Gilmour

Copyright © 2015 Eric William Gilmour
ENJOYING THE GOSPEL
Eric William Gilmour
Sonship International
P.O. Box 196281 Winter Springs, Fl. 32719
"Bringing the church into deeper experience of God in their daily lives."

Email: Eric@sonship-international.org
Website: www.sonship-international.org
Twitter/@sonshipintl
Facebook/sonshipintl
YouTube/ewgilmour

Printed in the United States of America

ISBN: 978-0-9898071-2-8

All rights reserved. No part of this document may be reproduced or transmitted in any form, by any means (electronic, photocopying, recording, or otherwise) without the written permission of the author.

Scripture quotations taken from the New American Standard Bible®. Copyright © 1960, 1962, 1963, 1968, 1971, 1972, 1973, 1975, 1977, 1995 by The LockmanFoundation Used by permission. (www.Lockman.org)

Cover Design by Jim McMahel
Copyright © 2015

Special Thanks to my dear friend and miracle editor Christiana Lacroix – you are an unseen hero.

The revelation of God and His divine government that the gospel introduces into our lives brings about an enjoyment beyond any earthly measure. The realities of enjoying the Triune God and the establishing of the gospel of His Kingdom are forever fused into one another. Eric is a man I believe God has truly entrusted with this message in for our generation in these last days.

David Popovici
KINGDOM GOSPEL MISSION

Eric Gilmour has the unique gift to bring revelation and fresh insight to classic subjects. His writings are an overflow of a rich inner life and are a gift to the reader enabling them to partake of the grace on his life.

Daniel Kolenda
CHRIST FOR ALL NATIONS

Eric Gilmour amazes me with his ability to teach while never ceasing to be a student. His grasp of the gospel's heartbeat is found in his love exchange with the Father, that he lets others have a glimpse of. I deeply appreciate all the resources of his heart laid out on paper.

Pastor Tyrone Gray
EDGE CHURCH

Eric Gilmour has become the message that he shares. The words you will find on the pages that follow are not some abstract truth that he has seen, distant and untouchable, but rather, the reality of Jesus can be seen, known, and experienced in the word of the Lord that Eric communicates, because Jesus Himself has been embraced and is being enjoyed by Eric.

Michael Dow
BURNING ONES INTERNATIONAL

Few people I know have a burning pursuit and passion like Eric to take advantage of this divine invitation into this real oneness with God Himself. I have watched Eric violently press into deeper realms of experience and revelation as his heart burned to KNOW GOD. Allow Eric's life and words to propel you into a deeper satisfaction in Christ as you become possessed by the Lord Himself!

Scott Howe
EVOKE MINISTRIES

No one that I know of display's the true expression of God's Voice and Presence in the earth like Eric Gilmour. He carries a razor sharp prophetic edge accompanied by an undeniable display of the Spirit's power. Most importantly everything about this man is without a doubt wholly buried and married into the fullness of Intimacy Divine...Jesus.

Brian Guerin
BRIDAL GLORY INTERNATIONAL

Eric Gilmour carries the Presence of the Master like few people I have met.

Michael Koulianos
JESUS IMAGE

CONTENTS

PREFACE ix
INTRODUCTION xiii
THE GOSPEL OF THE SPIRIT 1
THE GOSPEL OF EXPERIENCE 11
THE GOSPEL OF LIFE 21
THE GOSPEL OF PRESENCE 33
THE GOSPEL OF COMMUNION 41
THE GOSPEL OF COMMUNION II 53
THE GOSPEL OF JESUS 69
APPENDIX - DRAW NEAR 79
SPIRITUAL MAXIMS 85

"The Gospel is the offering of God's presence to Men."

> "In the presence of the Lord is fullness of Joy…"
> -Psalm 16:11

I dedicate this book to the only Omniscient, Omnipresent, and Omnipotent Being who reigns both now and forever; He is the wonder-filled I AM who has given to us His Son, Jesus, the only face of God, who manifests Himself to us through the presence of the Holy Spirit.
I am Yours and You are mine.
Come live Your life through me.

Preface

Preface

Ruth Heflin in her book *Glory* wrote,

"*As we were opening the service, Karen Stage, one of our girls, gave a word...there was a sound of eternity in her voice that was so glorious. It brought with it a refreshing. It was as if we all had taken a month's vacation in one second. She brought eternity into that meeting with the sound of her voice. It was a sound of glory that filled our souls and energized us.*"

May you experience what Ruth Heflin described and may it create in your soul an overwhelming desire to delight in God more than ever before in your life. May the breath of God fill your heart as you read this book.

I have included a prophetic speaking from Lindell Cooley; this particular excerpt is from a prophecy that took place during the Brownsville Revival in Pensacola, Florida from 1995-2000. This short inspired word encapsulates what my heart wants to convey in writing this book.

"*You're tired. You're tired of the battle. The reason you're weary is because you pulled away from Me. You've kept everything going but you have gone to your own devices and your own ways to make things happen. I Am the Lord God Almighty; just one word from Me causes all your enemies not only to tremble but to flee and run and be* divided. Don't forget Me, My son. Don't forget Me, My daughter. I am your refuge. I am your strength. Without Me you are no match for your enemy, but through Me all things are possible, because I'm able to subdue nations. I'm able to subdue your enemies and confuse them. Rest in Me. Return to Me with all your heart. Lay down your selfish ambition. Lay down your pride and come to Me just like a little child. I'll strengthen you and I will deliver you out of your trouble. Come to Me. Whoever wishes, come and drink of the water of life freely."

Introduction

In this silence I sit still and stay
For there will be much noise today
In the quiet here, I adore you
Before I ever set my hand to do
In this silence, stillness - all alone,
I prepare my heart to be thy throne

Summer 2014
Orlando, Florida

Introduction

If there is a room in the corridors of glory, in which Christ collects things precious to His heart, I am most certain that He has not gathered sermons, testimonies or snap shots of a man's ministry highlights. If Christ were to take me by the hand into that precious room, He might take me to a trenching shovel. I might look at Him and say, "What is this?" To which He would smile and reply, "This is the shovel upon which your tears fell as you worshipped Me in the heat of the day surrounded by devils; you were without one ministry opportunity, without any personal ambition but to love Me. Do you remember? I remember."

I believe God has placed value upon things that seem insignificant to men. It seems that He will establish those who give themselves so completely over to Him that they are no longer concerned with ever being established at all. He holds precious to His heart a life of intimate communion with Him that seeks nothing but Him. He cherishes a life that isn't motivated and inspired by "service" or "results" but is completely satisfied by His whisper and nearness, even in the midst of the mundane things in life. As C.S. Lewis simply but brilliantly stated, "God doesn't want something *from* us, He simply wants us." Dear reader, can I submit to you that God's ultimate desire is your heart?

The church needs to have a whole new perspective of what God deems a worthy response to His indescribable sacrifice. In these days that we live in, to enjoy the gospel seems like a foreign concept. We are overcome with our desires to see results and frustrated by our attempts to accomplish giant feats for God. I am not against massive results and or grand vision at all. However, it is imperative that such endeavors have their origin in and are sustained by the secret whisper of His presence.

One of my dearest friends in the entire world, Daniel Kolenda, is one of the most successful evangelists to ever live. At the time of this writing he has not only personally witnessed over 10 million people come to the Lord by way of mass crusade evangelism, but he has watched the gospel heal thousands of irreversible sicknesses and disabilities including multiple dead people coming back to life. Even with all these successes, he showed his true heart by these words: "After the crowds have come and gone and hundreds of thousands have been won to the Lord, I sit on my bed in that hotel room and it is still only God that satisfies."

I am not trying to stop believers from accomplishment; rather I just want to emphasize that anything that has significance to God must issue from Him, His presence, His voice.

Introduction

The true heart of the matter is the enjoyment of this glorious gospel: *the King of Glory offers His own blissful and empowering presence to men.* We must understand that such satisfaction is not merely a perk of God's presence in our lives but rather the means by which He frees and empowers us to obey Him. A Church that is not satisfied with God testifies to the world that God is not enough.

Dear reader, we must reconsider our motives, our love, and our focus as Christians, for the crucial sum of all things is that He is a living individual to be continually experienced and interacted with; He must be the preeminent satisfaction and empowerment of our lives. If He is not, we run the risk of falling into that hollow counterfeit that claims more souls than anything: empty, dry, cold and lifeless religion. How many powerful, gifted, successful ministers do not know God intimately? How many professing Christians claim to live by the power of the Holy Spirit, but have no real interactive fellowship with Him? And how many non-believers are chased away by a weak and joyless Church?

Our inspiration is our past experiences with Him; our satisfaction must be our present experience with Him; our hunger is for our future experiences with Him. I would much rather touch Him than attempt to define

Him. I would rather move Him than seek to simply understand Him. I would rather know Him than merely perform His works. Are you with me?

Chapter One
THE GOSPEL OF THE SPIRIT

"…(God's) goal was not simply to fit individuals for heaven but to create a people who by the power of the Spirit lived out the life of the future (the life of God Himself) in the present age…The Spirit as the experienced, empowering return of God's own personal presence in and among us, Who enables us to live as a radically eschatological people in the present world while we await the consummation."

-Gordon Fee
Paul the People and the Spirit of God

Chapter One: The Gospel of the Spirit
"...we were all made to drink of one Spirit."
-1 Corinthians 12:13

During the time that I write this, there is much controversy over what the Gospel actually is. Many conflicts, disputes and debates have occurred because of this essential subject. There are numerous men far more qualified than I to address such a matter, and in the midst of this contention, my heart in writing this book is not to communicate the specifics of the Gospel message, nor is it to bring correction or to expose false gospels. I only wish to articulate God's intention, which is for men to receive and enjoy the Gospel.

The Gospel at its most fundamental explanation is the reconciliation of God to a man who 1) repents of his sin that separates him from God by 2) trusting in the death, burial, resurrection and ascension of Jesus Christ, God's Son and 3) looks to Christ's return to earth to reign from Jerusalem over the world.

It is my deep conviction that the essence of the Gospel is man's reconciliation with God, namely, *the restoration of God and man finding pleasure in each other.* What does this mean? It means that the relationship which was disrupted and lost through Adam's (the first created man) disobedience has been restored to men through faith in the finished substitutionary work of the One God-man, Jesus Christ. Union between God and man experienced through interactive fellowship is the heart of the Gospel. The good news is that He has brought us back into Himself to enjoy the sweet communion and harmony that He enjoys in His Trinitarian self.

Dear reader, do you understand that the Gospel means that we have been invited into the bliss of the Godhead? To live in, through, and by the sweet union experienced by God Himself? His love is unmatched. He has freely given Himself to us even though we have all rejected Him outright. He alone is worthy of all our hearts and lives. God's paramount desire is to bring men into Himself and place Himself into men. I cannot emphasize it enough: *the Gospel is God offering His own presence to men.* To reject His presence is to reject the empowering, blissful satisfaction of His person from our lives.

What a gospel! We not only can recognize our depraved state without Him, but we can call on Him in response to the wonderful revelation of His love displayed on the cross. This wonderful gospel isn't just how we are made alive but is the means by which we live. Read it again: *we don't just live because of the Gospel, we live by the Gospel.*

Chapter One: The Gospel of the Spirit

The Gospel must be let into every part of our lives. The gospel disposition—a humble gaze upon God—must enter into our hearts in prayer, in relationships, in ministry, and every other aspect of our lives so that God's sweet presence may be welcomed as our life source.

Now, I wish to emphasize the Gospel of the Spirit, which is to say, how we experience this glorious gospel. As Gordon Fee wrote, "We must not merely cite the creed, but believe and experience the presence of God in the person of the Spirit." The Gospel is the only door through which the presence of the Holy Spirit will pass, and to live in His presence means that we must forever look to Him in helpless dependency, just like the first time we touched Him. "As you received Him so walk in Him (Colossians 2:6)."

After the devastating death of the Messiah, all the disciples fled, just as Jesus told them they would. Three days later, Mary Magdalene went to the tomb alone and made the earth-shattering discovery that the stone had been rolled away and the tomb was left empty. In the midst of what was probably absolute emotional confusion, she saw who she thought was the gardener and asked him where he had "taken her Lord" (John 20:13). When Jesus said her name, she immediately knew that it was Him and she wanted to throw her arms around Him. But Jesus said something very interesting to her, something that has perplexed me for a long time: "do not cling to me, for I have not ascended." (verse 17)

I believe that understanding what Jesus communicated through this statement is very important to experiencing and enjoying the fullness of the gospel, for the Gospel in its completeness includes the fact that He ascended into Heaven. The reason that He tells her that He did not want her to cling to Him was because He had "not yet ascended;" this should immediately turn our attention to the reason He would ascend in the first place, which will show us the reason why He forbade her from clinging to Him.

Jesus told the disciples that "if I do not go, the Spirit will not come" (John 16:7). John 7 tells us that the Spirit had not yet been given because Jesus had not yet been glorified, which took place when He ascended. It is safe to say that the primary reason for Jesus to ascend was to be glorified and to send the Spirit. How amazing that Jesus would ascend to send!

According to the Old Testament prophecies concerning the New Covenant, the reception of the Spirit was the core of His promise:

Chapter One: The Gospel of the Spirit

Isaiah 44:3 "For I will pour water on him who is thirsty, and floods on the dry ground; I will pour My Spirit on your descendants..."

Ezekiel 36:25-28 "Then I will sprinkle clean water on you, and you shall be clean; I will cleanse you from all your filthiness and from all your idols. I will give you a new heart and put a new spirit within you; I will take the heart of stone out of your flesh and give you a heart of flesh. I will put My Spirit within you and cause you to walk in My statutes, and you will keep My judgments and do them."

Joel 2:28-32 "And it shall come to pass afterward that I will pour out My Spirit on all flesh..."

It seems that, like Mary, much of modern Christianity has chosen to cling to the excitement of knowing the forgiveness of sins, to the joy of burying our old life and rising up in the new life we have in the death and resurrection of the Son. But Jesus would not have us embrace Him as the crucified and resurrected Son alone. He longs for something far more than just the forgiveness of our sins, the renunciation of our old life, and our walking in a new life. These are only the foundation upon which the fullness of the Salvation He purchased for us is built.

Dear reader, God's desire is to fill you with Himself. Every void in man God originally intended to fill with Himself. If Salvation is anything, it is God saving us from life and eternity apart from His presence, so He sent His very own Spirit into our hearts. It is this Holy Spirit that is God's presence in the world today. God gives His person and presence to us in the most intimate way: He fills us on the inside and mixes with our being so that we may live in union with Him; He wants to live through us by us living by Him.

The Gospel is incomplete without the sending of the Spirit into the hearts of men. I would venture to say that this is the heart of the Gospel, because the happiness and power in our lives comes from the Spirit of God who is the presence of God. Yes, it is 100 percent true that Jesus died in our stead to take away our sins by His blood. Yes, it is 100 percent true that He was buried to lay in death our old self. Yes, it is 100 percent true that He rose from the dead so that we may rise in newness of life with Him. But it is equally true that He ascended so that we might receive His Holy Spirit into our very being. This is the complete Gospel.

Please hear my heart cry as you read these words: *the gospel is the offering of God's presence to men.* His Spirit is everything! Without Him nothing lives. If we walk with Him we will not rebel against Him. If we do not walk with Him, we can only rebel against Him. He

Chapter One: The Gospel of the Spirit

puts right desires in us by His Spirit. He, by His Spirit, causes us to walk in His own ways.

The activity and resolve of man are simply at the surface of the human life. What lies beneath resolve is desire and nature but only the receiving of the Spirit can plunge such depths to transform these desires of the old nature. Otherwise men will vainly search inside themselves for a strength that they do not have to operate in a nature that they do not possess. Religion causes us to strive for outward conformity to Godliness, but all the while we fight against what we are; this will always lead to a frustrating dead end.

But the Holy Spirit has been sent to change all of this. Our new nature is literally the presence of God in our very being, strengthening us with a life we never had before and transforming our inward intent by mixing ourselves with God's actual nature. This is the Gospel of the Spirit.

Enjoying The Gospel

Chapter Two
THE GOSPEL OF EXPERIENCE

"The early Church did not preach much doctrine; they preached Christ. They had little to say of truths about Christ; it was Christ Himself...O for the Christ of Mary Magdalene, rather than the Christ of the critical theologian; give me the wounded body of divinity, rather than the soundest system of theology. We need Christ, not an abstract, doctrinal, pictured Christ but a real Christ. I may preach to you many a year, and try to infuse into your souls a love of Christ; but until you can feel that He is a real man and a real person, really present with you, and that you may speak with Him and tell Him of your needs, you will not readily attain to a love like that of the text, "You whom my soul loves."

-Charles Spurgeon

Chapter Two: The Gospel of Experience

"...He called you through our gospel, that you may gain the glory of our Lord Jesus Christ."
- 2 Thessalonians 2:14

It is necessary that I make a few remarks before we enter into this chapter. In no way am I suggesting any kind of sexual connection with God or any perverted sensual gratification in our bodies through this writing. I am simply drawing a parallel between what we can see in the book of Song of Solomon: that the bride is both representative of the church as a whole and of the individual believer's soul. I am pointing to the realities of what Paul the Apostle referred to in Ephesians 5 likening Christ and the Church to a husband and a wife. This is simply a symbolic means of communicating the incommunicable touch of God in the human soul.

Mike Bickle once wrote, "...experiencing God is not an option." If we are to have any authentic relationship with God as we as Christians claim, experience is crucial. I cannot take experience out of my relationship with God any more than I could reduce my marriage to a photo. My marriage is highly experiential, sound, touch, voice, presence, work, joy, pleasure and much more. If I take experience out of my relationship with God, than all I have left is an idea.

In speaking about experiencing the Gospel, let me be as candid as I possibly can: *Nobody gets pregnant holding hands;* it is simply impossible. There must be an intimate encounter and physical transference in order for conception to ever transpire. Many Christians, if not most, are literally holding hands with Jesus side by side, yet there is very little to no real intimate experience of Him; true reception of His word in the sweetness of His presence is rare.

So many merely have new lifestyles and new terminology; meet with new friends and listen to different music; struggle with the things that we used to as heathen and feel bad when we sin, this is due to a lack of a deeper sense of God in our everyday lives. I am afraid that too many are content to experience Him only in the public place, but conception only happens in the private place. If I could speak even more candidly, there are certain things that I will only do with my wife when we are alone. So it is with the heavenly bridegroom: He will only perform certain things when the door is shut and the heart of His beloved is fixated only on Him.

Many people wonder why they are not pregnant with God's purposes, or why they cannot give birth to those dreams that come from His heart. They are perplexed as to why they cannot overcome sin or see the fruit of the Spirit consistently in their lives. The

Chapter Two: The Gospel of Experience

sad fact is that even in midst of the "intimacy movement," many have merely adopted the language but will not truly live a life that is centered on His presence. But just as a pregnant woman cannot hide the fact that she has been with a man, union with God cannot be hidden. And no one can reflect a light brighter than what they have actually seen themselves. We must experience Him ourselves.

It is important to note that *no one gets pregnant reading "What To Expect When You're Expecting."* Just in case you are not familiar with this book, it is a large volume on the effects of being pregnant. A woman could memorize such an in-depth work but it will never inseminate her. There are many believers who live this way: they think that if they memorize and study the Bible, they will somehow find union with God and receive the infusion of His divine substance. It is purely impossible. Man needs to receive God's Words through the Scriptures and other means such as visions and impressions, in the sweetness of His presence alone with Him, where no eye can see.

It should go without saying that *no one gets pregnant by telling themselves that they are pregnant.* But we have whole movements based upon reminding yourself of who you are in Christ, speaking things into being, or simply "right believing." Our mental acrobatics cannot perform the miracle of sweet intimacy with

Jesus. It seems that our human mind will come up with anything to substitute a genuine face-to-face love exchange with God in His presence.

No one can get pregnant by desiring a child. Desire alone will never create union or the miracle that results from that union. Let me just add here that having children is not the *purpose* of intimacy but the *result* of intimacy. In the same way, God is intimate with us because He loves us, not so that we would produce offspring. We must consider that the inevitable result of intimacy will be productivity, but it is never the purpose. Intimacy unites us with Him so that our works issue out of what *we are through union with Him*.

If fruitfulness were the purpose of intimacy and not the result of this love union, than God would not be looking for a bride; He would be searching for a surrogate. On the flip side, if man looks to God for power and results alone, then ministry has become a mistress instead of his offspring of love union with His God. Everything in God is all about the mingling brought by the sweet intimate reception of His word in the bliss of His presence.

No one will become fruitful in this life simply because he or she has a great desire to be. There are whole movements based on "crying out" and fasting[1] and frustrated pleading with God for something to happen. But, dear reader, this is so important for me to pass on to you: the interactive fellowship with the Spirit is our uniting experience with God, not our desire for it.

Along the same lines, *no one gets pregnant by commitment alone;* otherwise, my wife would have become pregnant the moment we said, "I do." God has given us such great parallels in our daily living of the life He wants to share with us, and marriage is a powerful one. But commitment to someone doesn't automatically mean that you are intimate with them. Though commitment is a beginning, it is still possible to be married and not be intimate.

Let me interject here that the reason why so many people know very little about the ecstasies of God is because they have no commitment to Him. Fornication is sin because it is the expression of covenant without covenant. In essence, we are telling God that other things are more important to us than our relationship with Him. Before God will overshadow you with the blissful intimate experience of His nearness, there must first be a settling in a man's heart that *all other loves are refused.* As is stated

---

[1] I must note that fasting is a legitimate part of any real thirst for God.

in marriage ceremonies all over the world, "…forsaking all others, keeping only to thee." God will not pour His Spirit into a man who is not fully His.

Yes, commitment is fundamental but some people really believe that because they are willing to die for Christ and His cause they are becoming like Him. But this is not the case; a man needs the presence of God to unfold the living voice of God into His soul. And those whose lives are truly His will give themselves to experiencing Him every day.

Lastly, *no one can become pregnant by knowing the "methods"* by which to do so. Without getting too explicit, one can know every way to be intimate and yet not experience intimacy with another person. Just because we can teach about prayer and have learned everything concerning the intimate life, it doesn't mean that we are living by that ecstatic experience ourselves. Experiential union comes from experiential fellowship alone.

This is the desire that burns in my heart: for the church to come into a deeper awareness, consciousness and experience of God's presence in their daily lives. There is simply no substitute for it. So let me say that quote from Mike Bickel one more time, "experiencing God is not an option." This issue

Chapter Two: The Gospel of Experience

is life and death. A life of experiencing God is authentic salvation. This is the abundant life.

Enjoying The Gospel

Chapter Three
THE GOSPEL OF LIFE

"God's intention for man is not a matter of doing, but a matter of eating. If man eats well and eats rightly, then he will be right. God's intention is not that we serve Him, do good to please Him. God's intention is that we eat Him. He came that we may eat Him. He came to present Himself to us as life in the form of food. We have to take Him as food by feeding upon Him and eating Him. After receiving Him, the problem is not related to work, to service…but to eating. How do you eat, what do you eat and how much do you eat? God's intention is that man would simply take God Himself as his food. That man would feed on God."

-Witness Lee, **The Tree of Life**

Chapter Three: The Gospel of Life

"As the living Father sent Me, and I live because of the Father, so he who eats Me, he also will live because of Me."
-John 6:57

In the 6th chapter of the book of John we read that when Jesus saw the crowds "coming to Him" (verse 2) the first thing He said was, "Where can we buy bread so that these may eat" (verse 5). Immediately after this He orders those who have come to Him to "sit down" and it quickly follows that "He distributed *to them who were seated*" (verse 11).

I want us to recognize that when we "come to Him," Jesus' initial concern is for our nourishment; His first thought is, "I want to feed you." But in order for Him to be able to satisfy us with Himself, we must first "be seated." This speaks to us of rest, of stillness, of relaxing. Just as the Psalmist says, He makes you to, "lie down in green pastures. He leads [you] beside still waters."(Psalms 23:2) The term "still waters" could be more literally translated as "waters of rest" or refreshment. God will not chase a man down in an attempt to feed Him. Only those who have come to Him in an attitude of rest will receive and eat. Do you recall Mary and Martha? God did not make Martha stop serving, but at the same time He only gave His words to Mary.

Here in John 6 we see Jesus telling those who have come to Him, hungry, to "sit down." This is an order, a command, if you will, that is tied together with His desire to feed them. He says, "Rest!" because He simply cannot and will not feed the man who will not rest—that man who refuses to relinquish all of his cares, activities and efforts to wait upon the Lord in simple trust. That is why the Scriptures are clear to point out that *He gave* to "them that were seated." We must obey this serious command from the Lord if we are to partake of the bread that both He Himself *is* and *gives*.

It is significant that Christ Himself gave the bread, which means that the bread issued out from His person and presence. The Old Testament calls the bread in the tabernacle, "the bread of the presence." Christ dispenses Himself as bread to those who will relinquish themselves to Him, those who will put their efforts aside and simply come to Him. Many people are pressing and working and fighting to get God to give them something of Himself, but it will not happen. We must recognize His desire to feed us, obey His command to rest and then receive in His presence that supernatural bread from His own hand.

Once I had short break at work and was looking for a place to eat my lunch. The only place I could find was a long picnic table occupied by several young people

Chapter Three: The Gospel of Life

with books. I shamelessly joined them at the table and quickly found out that they were culinary students studying and sharing recipes from their cookbooks. As I watched and listened, I perceived something: in the midst of their pictures, conversations, opinions and knowledge about food, not one of them actually had any food at all.

Dear reader, this simple story brings to life a major issue that is dangerous to the Church. Talk, study, books, materials, and knowledge we have, yet too many of us are starving to death with memorized recipes and cookbooks. We memorize Scripture and cling to our Bibles with dogmatic belief, yet we stumble about malnourished and lifeless like the rest of the world. Sadly, this describes a large part of the Church. If I found a man dying of hunger, I wouldn't be able to save him by giving him recipes or describing food to him. Even the greatest chef in the world will die if he doesn't eat food; he cannot draw an ounce of sustenance from his knowledge, experience, materials, books or teachings. Men are dying in their marriages, suffering in their addictions and wasting away from a lack of faith as they look to ink and paper alone for salvation. Man's desperate need is actual nourishment.

So here comes Jesus, who calls Himself the "bread that COMES down from heaven" (verse 41). He is the bread that "came down" and the bread that "comes down." There is a continual coming, or shall I say an endless begetting, of the Son by the Father. We do not live just because we ate Him at one time; we must live our lives by eating Him.

What does it mean *to eat*? It means to *receive nourishment*.

What does it mean to be *nourished*? It is *to be sustained and supplied with all that is needed for life, health and growth.*

In Matthew 22:2 Jesus likens the Kingdom of Heaven to a feast. A feast is a celebratory time set aside to receive nourishment by eating. We have been invited to a life of feasting upon Jesus, a life of enjoying Christ as our nourishment. The way of living in the Kingdom of God is receiving all that is needed for our Spiritual life, health and growth by eating the Bread of Heaven.

In this Kingdom banquet, Christ is both that which is celebrated and consumed. He Himself gives us Himself as Spiritual life and Spiritual health. He is the means by which we grow. He is our nourishment or all that is needed for:

Chapter Three: The Gospel of Life

- **Life** – He is a living experience (by His presence and voice) and our life-supply.

- **Health** – The quality of our internal life is in exact proportion to our reception of His life (voice and presence). Many Christians are alive, but they are sick. For they have not gained their daily nourishment from Christ who is our life. Men eat other things, not knowing that these substitutes for the True Bread are killing them.

- **Growth** – Our maturity, expansion, and union with His life are wholly dependent upon receiving Him as our life. As we receive Him into ourselves He will permeate and illuminate us, causing us to grow in strength and health.

Is there a better picture of oneness and spiritual empowerment than eating Him? There is no greater practice of oneness with Him than enjoying Him. To reiterate these points, the life we have received because we ate Him is sustained by continually eating Him. The maturity of divine life in us is wholly dependent upon the continuous reception of that same life.

Jesus parallels His own life in this world, dependent on the power of the Father, with our own earthly lives, which should be empowered by eating of Him.

God was Christ's life source and He is ours. Jesus said, "Man will not live by bread alone, but by every word that proceeds out of the mouth of God" (Matthew 4:4). In other words:

$$Bread = Word = Life.$$

He, as the Bread of life, is that Speaking from God that must be received as our life source. John the revelator calls Jesus the "Word of Life" (1 John 1). Our life source is His speaking/voice. He is the living Speaking of God and our nourishment for a godly home, relationship, mouth, heart, employment, ministry and life. Without His voice, we are empty and lifeless. David said, "If you are silent to me, I will become like those who go down to the pit" (Psalm 28:1). The digression of every Christian life starts at this point, with the loss of His voice.

Ask yourself, "Do I hear Him in my life?" Let me illustrate the major difference between learning and hearing with this example: I used to prepare crab legs in the kitchen when I worked at the Pelican's Perch in Pensacola, Florida, but I couldn't tell you what one tastes like because I have never eaten one. You see, all the facts in the world about cooking crabs and all my outward contact with them in preparing them for others to eat never acquainted me with their taste. So it is with experiencing God; theologians across the

Chapter Three: The Gospel of Life

globe have defined Him but they have never eaten Him. Because of this, their heads are heavier than their hearts; while their brains are full their souls are hollow.

"Religion," in the negative sense of the word, is lifeless devotion to God. It is seeking to live in a way that pleases God by our own efforts. Dietrich Bonheoffer once wrote, *"Adam's curse was having to live life before God without life from God."* Men cannot live for God without life from God. Religion is the slavery of efforts and striving; it is and will always be focused on "might and power." But true Christianity is a Spiritual thing and cannot be lived through the energy of men. We must eat Spiritual food if we are to ever live a Spiritual life. Religion is cold, dry, dead and empty; men suffocate under its power, for it presses upon men a Spiritual standard without any Spiritual power. I will say this phrase until I pass into the next life: religion demands for men to live according to a nature that they do not posses.

What is the answer for those people who have eaten Him at one time but are still living malnourished lives? The answer is a life of eating the Lord. Witness Lee wrote:

The result of eating God is that we express Him. After we enjoy the divine life we express the divine life. God is life and His Word is also life. This Word speaks, unfolds, reveals and expresses God...for the Lord Jesus to say that He is edible means that God Himself is edible. Therefore, we can boldly declare that God is edible and that we can partake Him, eat Him and digest Him...If we enjoy God as our nourishment, He will eventually become the constituent of our being. We must enjoy Christ as our life-supply.

You may ask, "What does this mean? How can I eat Him? I read the Bible. I pray. I go to church. I sing songs and worship Him. But how do I eat Him?" Let me help you understand what transforms our cookbooks into a delectable buffet: It is the presence of God. The presence of God passes the Word through out brains into our blood.

Jesus goes on to say, "Truly, truly, I say to you, unless you eat the flesh of the Son of Man and drink His blood, you have no life in yourselves. He who eats My flesh and drinks My blood has eternal life... For My flesh is true food, and My blood is true drink. He who eats My flesh and drinks My blood abides in Me, and I in him."(verses 53-55)

I apologize for suggesting something so elementary, but in order to eat something *you must be in its presence.* Is this too simple point out? I really don't think so because it teaches us that the most

Chapter Three: The Gospel of Life

fundamental aspect of receiving this Spiritual nourishment is the sweet presence of God. Without His presence the letters in the bible stay on the page, but in His presence, they are written in your heart. In His presence God becomes audible, tangible, visible, and yes, even edible to our hearts! If we do not have His presence we cannot eat Him, and if we do not eat Him we have "no life in ourselves." These four words make a statement of the true state of our being without Him; we truly have "no life in ourselves."

In verse 53, Jesus brings together two wonderful realities of the Christian life: eating Him and abiding in Him. He who eats abides and He who doesn't eat doesn't abide. The way we abide in the divine life is by feasting upon Him.

I once asked my friend, Dr. Jeff Hubing, who is a New Testament scholar, about the tense of the phrase, "he who eats me." His response was enlightening: "The better way to understand that phrase would be to say, *the eating one.*" We must realize that living and eating are as contingent upon each other in our Spiritual life as they are in our physical life. That is the teaching of Jesus. As Witness Lee continues, "The Christian life is a life of daily experiencing the Christ we have received. The Christian life is a life of experiencing Jesus all the time."

Men constantly tell me, "You cannot live by experience." But my response will always be the same: "Without experience we don't live."

Chapter Four
THE GOSPEL OF HIS PRESENCE

"My heart cries unto You by still desires without voice, and my silence speaks unto You...Come, Lord, come, for without You I have no glad day nor hour for You are all my joy, and without You my soul is barren and void. I am a wretch, and in prison, and bound with fetters, till You, through the light of Your gracious presence, visit me and refresh me, and bring me again to liberty and choose to show Your favorable and loving countenance unto me. Let others seek what they will, but truly there is nothing that I will seek, or that will please me, but You... speak inwardly to my soul..."

-Thomas A. Kempis, "Imitation of Christ" (MT Vernon, Pauper Press: 1872) p. 111

Chapter Four: The Gospel of His Presence

"Come to Me all you who are weary and heavy laden and I will give you rest. Take My yoke upon you and learn of Me for I am meek and lowly in heart and you will find rest for your souls. For My yoke is easy and My burden is light."
- Matthew 11:28

Such an invitation from the mouth of Christ, God's prefect expression, carries such beauty that it stands as one of the most comforting statements we find in the Scriptures. The fact that this invitation is extended to "all" is a wonderful expression of God's kindness and love, for *anyone who will come to Him*, He will never reject. It is for certain that the more we experience Him, the more this universal and continual invitation will consume our thoughts and cause all of our other interests to literally wither away. For me personally, this is the phrase that Jesus says to me every day of my life: *"Come to Me..."*

The phrase "Come to Me" in its most basic understanding means entering into His presence. Jesus calls to everyone suffering under the weariness and heaviness of this life so He can offer us relief and rest. It is clear to me that our weariness in this life has its roots in the lack of His presence, and our heaviness is rooted in self-reliance. A life of rest from fear, worry, pain, striving, sin, and oppression is a life of continually coming unto Jesus. Note that *all of our weariness will melt away when we come to Him.*

The presence of Jesus frees us from the constant stress that the tick of time puts upon the soul; this is called rest. The presence of Jesus frees us from the constant frustration of desire that brews in the soul; this is called rest. Our senses are constantly bombarded by our surroundings but the presence of Jesus frees us from their influence; this is called rest. It is in the presence of Jesus that we are free from striving and we realize that God will perform all things through us. This is called rest. Rest is the ceasing of natural activity for the ignition of divine activity. The life of rest is the life that waits to be empowered by God's living Word. Obedience is when a man's life is yielded to the extent that God can perform through that man the things He has spoken to that man.

This heavenly bliss and freedom in His presence is not a lottery; it is rather a promise. Jesus died for our sins and was beaten for our sickness, but He came and died to close the distance between ourselves and God. It is the work of the cross that makes this wonderful and cognizant presence available to us.

In the next breath, He who says, "Come to me..." says, "Take my yoke upon you..." Throughout the gospels, Jesus constantly teaches the fundamental Kingdom reality that our liberation is His presence. At the core of this freedom is being rescued from the tyranny of self-rule. We were not made to rule ourselves—our

Chapter Four: The Gospel of His Presence

self-management is too feeble, too flawed and too flimsy to sustain life. If a man is left to himself, he destroys himself because the natural inclination of man is death. But God is the source of life and His rule contains only that which He is Himself. His yoke is His wonderful rule and it is far lighter than any other.

Jesus uses the word, "easy." Many of us love to speak about how difficult our lives are or how terrible the things are that happen to us for Jesus sake; but His "yoke is easy." No matter what is happening to us, we can find divine ease when we come into His presence and yield to His dominion simply because He will carry every load through us. Even in the heart of suffering, there is a fellowship with Him that gives us peace that passes all understanding. This means that He promises to give us peace when it doesn't make any natural sense.

Richard Wurmbrand suffered in Romanian prisons for 14 years, 7 years of which were spent in solitary confinement. He said this about his years of torture: "The bride was in the embraces of the heavenly bridegroom. We received His Holy Kiss. We knew His caresses. It has been one of the most beautiful times of my life."

When we yield to Jesus' eternal rule and put on His light and easy yoke, our hearts become conditioned in meekness and humility, through which He dispenses His rest into our lives, regardless of any life situation. Meekness and humility are inseparable. The taking up of His yoke, the renunciation of our own self-rule, and the submission to His divine rule are man's humility and meekness.

We have a beautiful image of this sweet humility and meekness in the life of Christ. According to Philippians 2, He was obedient to the point of death. Each one of His choices to obey and submit to His Father teaches us the way of true humility. This kind of obedience is only the product of God's presence in a man. Such is the life of rest: at liberty from human rebellion and fear of death. There is no more unshackled life than the one that is laid at Jesus' feet. Whether or not the knife actually comes to our throat, we are His. And His presence is our joy and strength, peace and love.

Remember this: it is not the yoke of God that is heavy. Our sin and our self-management are heavy. Selfishness and pride wear out the saints and sentence humanity to death. Independence and self-sufficiency weigh down the heavy yoke of the self-life. Stubbornness causes men to reject Christ's easy

Chapter Four: The Gospel of His Presence

yoke. Such a man will never come to Jesus. Mark my words, *he will die of fatigue.*

Praise God! Jesus has called for all men who will, to come to Him—from any walk of life, under any hellish oppression, through any soul struggle—and enter His presence to find this God-ordained realm of rest. In humility come to Jesus today and every day; lay down your heavy yoke and pick up His easy one; let Him take your soul—restless and weary, burdened and heavy, tired and torn; allow Him to grant you rest and ease in His presence all the days of your life.

I will conclude this chapter with a wonderful description of the pleasure of His presence by John Ruusbroec. Let this make your heart salivate for the fullness of His presence that belongs to those who will humbly come to Him and take His yoke upon themselves:

"This sweetness gives rise to a feeling of delight in the heart and all the corporeal powers, so that a person thinks he is enveloped from within by a divine embrace of affection. This delight is greater and more pleasant for both soul and body than all the delights which earthly things could produce, even if a single person could enjoy them all together. In this delight God enters the depths of the heart with so much joy that the heart overflows from within. This

makes a person realize how miserable are those who live apart from obedience. This delight causes a melting of the heart, so that a person cannot contain Himself out of his interior joy.

This delight gives rise to a spiritual inebriation. Spiritual inebriation means that a person receives more perceptible delight than his heart or desire could long for or contain. Spiritual inebriation produces much strange behavior in a person. It makes a person become silent and melt away out of the delight he feels in all his senses.

Sometimes he wonders what is happening to him. On the level of our corporeal sensibility, this delight becomes so intense that it seems to such a person that his heart will break. Such a person should therefore with a humble heart glorify and praise the Lord who is able to do all this, and with fervent devotion he should thank Him for being willing to do it. He should constantly hold his heart and speak sincerely with his tongue these words, "Lord, I am not worthy of this, but I have great need for your fathomless goodness and strength." Through such humility he will be able to grow and increase in obedience.

Chapter Five
THE GOSPEL OF COMMUNION

"God wants every one of your senses to be alive unto Him. He wants you to be thrilled with the sound of His voice. He wants you to be thrilled with the touch of His hand. He wants you to be thrilled at the sight of His countenance. He wants you to be deeply moved by His presence, as He comes near."

-Ruth Heflin, GLORY page 118

Chapter Five: The Gospel of Communion

"...the fellowship of the Spirit, be with you all."
-2 Corinthians 13:14

Dear reader, if I was to ask you what God is after in your life, what would you say? Some would say obedience or faith or worship or love or something along these lines. I believe all of these are right answers, but God has a more specific yearning in His heart. He has a burning desire to reproduce His Son through the dispensing of the Spirit of His Son into us.

God's joyful objective is to transform us into the image of His Son. And believe me, you want this too, for every aspect of your being was made to be so deeply mixed with God. So mixed with Him that it is difficult to tell where one begins and the other ends. Every problem in the human life can be traced back to one area or another that has not been mingled with God.

That is what the Apostle Paul refers to when He writes, "the image of His Son." He uses such language only a few times in the Scriptures, the first mention is in Romans 8:29: "He predestined us to be *conformed to the image of His Son...*" The heart of God's desire is clearly explained here: the *"image of the Son."*

What does, "the image of His son" mean? It means that Christ's very person is unobstructed while living through us. Another Scripture that uses such language tells us how this is going to happen. 2 Corinthians 3:18 says, "…beholding as in a mirror the glory of the Lord, [we] are being transformed *into the same image* from glory to glory, just as from the Lord, the Spirit." It is plainly laid out that the image of Jesus through our being, or the person of Christ united with our being, is the result of gazing upon the ever increasing manifestation of God, who is the Lord Jesus Christ, experienced through the presence of the Holy Spirit.

If, as Paul has plainly shown, beholding the glory is the only way to be transformed into the image of the Son, then not beholding His glory causes us to remain in our own image. This brings me to the reason for this chapter on the Gospel of Communion.

The single most common question that I am asked, both in my travels and through social media, is, "How do I experience God?" Many times I will give the inquirer a short answer like, "The experience of God is so rare because scattered minds are so common. Get still." Or I'll respond with: "Just adore Him." The reason I can address the question with blanket statements like these is because our problem is a common one: We are a self-conscious people;

Chapter Five: The Gospel of Communion

everything in each of our individual little worlds revolves around us.

To give God all of our attention and affection will rip the soul away from the rule of self-consciousness and set it free to fly. Most people never soar in the heights because they are weighed down by the heaviness of self-rule. The soul's rebellion must be suffocated daily by wholehearted adoration through stillness. Oh mark these words in your soul; stillness is the antithesis of rebellion.

So many of us go into prayer and never actually touch God because we did everything but adore Him. Many people's spiritual senses are numbed in the closet by all the pressure they put on themselves to be there and accomplish something. *Our itch to accomplish something stems from our desire for something other than just Him.* I would read that last statement again.

Many have also asked, "How long should I pray?" Such a question is so difficult to answer because I know that man thinks clock while God thinks connection. We all have different lives and different schedules that God has entrusted to us in this life; some have more free time than others. Nevertheless, sitting with God is the most important thing in our lives.

Enjoying The Gospel

A mother once wrote and rebuked me for encouraging people to spend large quantities of time with God; she felt condemned that she didn't have enough uninterrupted time to block out for just being with Him. Now, I don't mean to step on anyone's toes, but no matter how busy you are, you are never going to be as busy as Jesus was: The crowds came from all over to simply be where He was; the sick continuously pulled at Him; He was always with the twelve. Yet He still got up before the sun and went to a solitary place to be with God.

John 8:1 "Everyone went to his home but Jesus went to the Mount of Olives."

Luke 6:12 "It was at this time that He went off to the mountain to pray and He spent a whole night in prayer…"

Luke 4:42 "Jesus left and went to a secluded place."

Mark 1:35 "In the early morning, while it was still dark, Jesus got up, left the house and went away to a secluded place and was praying there."

Luke 22:39 "He proceeded to the Mount of Olives, as was His custom."

Luke 5:16 "Jesus often slipped away to the wilderness to pray."

Chapter Five: The Gospel of Communion

Matthew 14:23 "He went up on a mountain side by Himself to pray..."

Luke 22:41 "He withdrew...and prayed."

Many people say that they have no time to sit in stillness and adoration before the Lord. But the funny thing is that they know a lot about "Dancing With The Stars," Fantasy Football, "Home and Garden" or some other trending thing. The truth is that what we do with our time is an uncomfortable exposing of our true spiritual state.

One time a woman wrote a well thought out letter rebuking me for calling people to spend time alone simply worshipping God. She said that she doesn't have an hour to herself. I thought to myself, with how long and well written this letter is, it must have taken her at least an hour to write. I guess that she had an hour to talk to me, but she hasn't an hour to talk with God? We as humans will do almost anything to justify our staleness.

Backsliding is when your heart stops aching for His presence. Most of us are living in this state right now, so used to our lukewarm hearts that any talk from a heart on fire with love is simply "impractical" or "radical" or "wishful thinking." But dear friend, let me encourage you to never cover the flame in your heart to comfort the ice in another's. We must call the church back to the Lover of her soul.

When I was in college at the Brownsville School of Ministry in Pensacola, Florida, it was easy to "live in the Glory." Not only did we live in the midst of an unparalleled sustained visitation of the Spirit, but also we had set aside our lives to just seek the Lord, learn the Scriptures, and preach the gospel. *We literally ate as little as we could and prayed as much as we could.* Our bodies wasted away, our teeth broke, our skin was pale, our relationships dwindled and we lost touch with modern society. It was like we had been frozen in time, as if we had created a bubble in which we set our faces to seek Him and nothing else. We were truly aliens in this world.

Of course this level of focused prayer and adoration was only for a season, and now everyone involved lives with pressing responsibilities, families, ministries and relationships that we must steward. Even so, I remember working construction sometimes 12 hours a day in the Florida sun, coming home to a wife and daughter, and having little time to get alone with God. When I saw what my schedule was like, I had to make a decision to get up hours before the sun to sit with Him. If I wasn't driving to the construction sites, I would sit in the back seat worshipping Jesus and meditating on the Scriptures. I would incorporate

Chapter Five: The Gospel of Communion

fasting into my life in ways that I could handle with my workload (i.e. every other day or 3 days a week to stay strong for manual labor). I would take some weekends and lock the door in my room to be alone from 4AM to 4PM so that I still had the late afternoon to help my wife and be with the kids. Any time my wife took the kids away to do something that I couldn't go to, I would literally stay in my closet every moment I was home including all weekend. On top of these things, I would look at my schedule and find a three-day, seven-day or sometimes ten-day window that I could block out, just to sit in my closet with a jug of water, to adore Him, to let Him lead me through the Scriptures. The ecstasies and blissful life changing encounters I had in those times are worth more to me than anything else in my life.

During this time I would wake up early, spend time in adoration, and then come into the office earlier than anyone else to kneel down, at each person's chair, and pray for them. I would pray that they would fall in love with Jesus. No one knew, but it wasn't for them to know. I was burning with a desire to be faithful to the stewardship God had entrusted me with in that work place, knowing that I have the power, privilege and responsibility of God's ear.

In another season of life, I worked at Christ for all Nations; my days were long and I had a two-hour commute back and forth every day. It was my habit to skip lunch and lock myself in an empty office to simply adore Jesus. Sometimes, I stayed late or came in early, along with taking the commute time, to pray in the Spirit over some glorious worship music or feed my spirit man listening to old messages from the voices of prophets.

Why am I telling you this? I only say these things to stir you to take seriously your life of communion with God and to make communion with God your life, and from that place to steward well whatever environment and relationships He has divinely situated for you at this present time of your life. This is what matters. Not crowds and what most would call "results" but honest stewardship of what is divinely right before you. I also want to encourage you that just because a daily experience of God has not been your life source up until now doesn't mean that it cannot be or that it is not supposed to be.

Concerning seeking the Lord, my Dear friend Daniel Kolenda says, "Our seeking of the Lord is in exact proportion to our value of Him." He goes on to say that if you were offered $1,000,000 to make a two hour window every day to sit alone with God, you would find a way, simply because the value of that money is so great. If you value God Himself as the reward of seeking Him, you will cut out whatever

Chapter Five: The Gospel of Communion

you must in order to simply lay upon His chest and listen to His heart beat. Remember that God is not responsible for an inconsistent experience of Him.

Though discipline is the beginning, as you experience the sweetness of His presence more and more, it will swallow up your soul and all other interests will wither away. Delight will soon swallow discipline. You never have to tell a couple that has fallen in love to make time to be with each other; it is all they think about. They simply live to be together, and to be apart from each other makes them feel as if they are each dying a slow torturous death. If you have ever been in love, the real kind that robs you of any social existence, you know what I am taking about. In the same way, to be in love with Jesus means to love being with Him. Love causes delight to devour discipline.

Chapter Six
THE GOSPEL OF COMMUNION PART 2

"Separation never comes from His side. He is always ready for communion with a prepared heart, and in this happy communion the bride becomes ever fairer, and more like her Lord. She is being progressively changed into His image, from one degree of glory to another, through the wondrous working of the Holy Spirit, until the Bridegroom can declare: Thou art all fair, My love; And there is no spot on thee. And now she is fit for service, and to it the Bridegroom woos her; she will not misrepresent Him…Union with Christ, and abiding in Christ, what do they not secure? Peace, perfect peace; rest, constant rest; answers to all our prayers; victory over all our foes; pure, holy living; ever-increasing fruitfulness. All, all of these are the glad outcome of abiding in Christ."

- **Hudson Taylor, Union and Communion**

Chapter Six: The Gospel of Communion Part 2

> *"...you were called into fellowship with His Son."*
> *-1st Corinthians 1:9*

Dear friends, everyone says, "God is all I want," but their lack of peace, joy and contentment testifies against them. Everyone says, "I love your presence." But you can tell how much someone really loves His presence by how uncomfortable they are when they are not aware of Him. Our schedule will testify more truly about what we love more than our mouths. How do we spend our time? We can tell how much we love His presence by how dependent we are upon Him throughout our day.

I want to write, step by step, how I experience the Lord every day. Though I know many of you reading this book already have deep relationships with God, I want to briefly walk through what I have found and believe to be the most important stages of prayer. Hopefully this will aid each of us in our daily experience of God.

The first stage in the soul that causes us to enter into an experience with God is **DEPRIVATION.** We must recognize our own personal depravity, meaning that we must recognize that it is impossible for us to make something happen when we are alone with Him. Our efforts are completely useless. One of the ways we can recognize this poverty of spirit is relaxation; when we relax, our inward disposition testifies to God that we really are impotent in and of ourselves. To relax means that we recognize our personal bankruptcy and that all of our own efforts are worthless. So we give up or surrender. We must recognize our deep and utter helplessness and simply cast ourselves upon Him.

The second stage in the soul that causes us to experience God is what I would call **CONCENTRATION,** which is another way of saying stillness. This is where we have, after recognizing our inability, collected ourselves and given our selves completely to God. Stillness doesn't mean we cannot move; it means that the activity of the mind outside of fixation upon Him is stopped and the affections of the heart are centered on God Himself. It is removing all of our attention from lesser things and refusing to be interrupted by wayward thoughts. Concentration, or stillness, is basically focusing all of one's attention upon God and away from other things. As we move into the next stage we will find that to be frozen in His sweetness is when the stillness we offer Him is swallowed by the stillness that comes from Him. God has this way about Him, as Psalm 65:7 describes: *"...Who stills the roaring of the seas, the roaring of their waves, and the tumult of the peoples."* Jesus, the exact representation of the Father, fulfilled this promise

Chapter Six: The Gospel of Communion Part 2

physically when the disciples were in turmoil on the sea. *"He got up and rebuked the winds and the sea, and it became perfectly calm."* (Matthew 8:26) So first we recognize our deprivation and then, with humility, we can enter concentration, which prepares our hearts for the next stage.

The third stage we must enter into to experience God is **ADORATION**. *This is the most important stage because the stages before lead up to it, and everything that comes after is a result of it.* After the soul has recognized its poverty and focused itself in stillness, then and only then can it offer itself up as a complete offering to God. Adoration is incomplete until our souls are still. Many of us have this problem: we are looking to the Lord while simultaneously worried about other things. We are split in two. There is no such thing as dualistic adoration. This is why men cannot touch Him, because Holy Spirit fire only falls on a whole sacrifice. Partial attentiveness will never receive the touch of God. The Scripture even states that, *"You will seek Me and find Me when you search for Me with all your heart (Jeremiah 29:13)."*

The first and greatest commandment given to us by Jesus and inscribed onto the heart of a man by the Spirit is, *"Love the Lord your God with all your heart."*(Matthew 22:37) Five hundred years before, David prayed that God would give him an undivided heart (Psalm 86:11). It is this wholehearted attentiveness that offers authentic adoration. Adoration is not a state of mind; it is the preoccupation of the soul with the beauty of the Lord. It is the purest form of seeking God, opening the valve of our receptivity and enabling us to cling to God. Adoration is like air in the Kingdom of God. This is the most indispensible element of the Christian life. It is both the enjoyment and the practice of our union with God, the exercise of our faith and the reception of His life which empowers us to obey. Adoration is the beginning, sustaining and end of all things in our union with God.

The fourth stage in the experience of God is **MANIFESTATION**. In adoration there will always be a manifestation of His presence. As we turn our attention to Him, it will take us like a river takes a yielded body. Oars are forbidden in the river of God (Isaiah 33:21).

When I first abandoned my life to the Lord in 1996, a man of God, picked me up early in the morning for a road trip. As I sat there in the passenger seat, he turned to me and said, "Let's pray." I immediately started to rattle off in tongues, progressively getting louder with fervency and focus. Anyone looking at me would think I was in agony, rocking back and forth in constant motion. This man of God waited

Chapter Six: The Gospel of Communion Part 2

patiently for me to finish machine-gunning God with tongues and desperate cries. When the smoke cleared from my war initiation with hell, the car became silent. Then with the steering wheel in one hand and his steaming coffee in the other, this man of God said softly, "Jesus, I worship you." He sat quietly and then said it again, "I worship you, precious Lamb of God." An in an instant, the whole car gradually filled with the undeniable presence of the Holy Spirit. The tangible glory of heaven began to touch my soul. I was frustrated; I was infuriated; I was intrigued by how God's presence was invoked with so much ease. This man didn't raise his voice or even appeal to God to manifest Himself; he simply looked to Jesus in adoration. I learned an incredibly valuable lesson that day, namely, that adoration is the secret to experiencing the manifestation of His presence. Oh dear reader, you must let this into your heart, a life of adoration is worth all the activity and power in the entire world. To gaze upon Him in sweet fixation and loving worship is more valuable to God than any spiritual gift or service. My favorite quote from A.W. Tozer would fit very well here, "when the eyes of the soul looking out meet the eyes of God looking in, heaven has begun upon the earth."

This next stage is very important. Many people reach the stage of manifestation, but the fifth stage in experiencing God is what separates the men from the boys: it is the state of **RESIGNATION,** it is literally the fermentation of the sweetness of God's presence into wine. Fermentation takes time, a specific kind of time, time resigned to His presence. As humans, we have a natural itch to move on, a desire for progress or momentum, but this robs so many people of the divine mixing of divinity with humanity. They are satisfied to touch and go. But resignation is lingering with Him, a simple acquiescence of oneself to the nothingness of God.

What do I mean by nothingness? This is when it seems that nothing is happening. The natural man is so fixed on activity that the nothingness of simple resignation to God's presence in still adoration is an irritation to him. We are addicted to activity and live by movement, therefore the still sweet nothingness of God will always be nonsense to our natural human nature. Too many of us wait for something to "happen" while we are in His presence without realizing that His presence *is* the happening. This stage of resigning to His presence will determine if you want anything other than just Him.

In a service at Brownsville Assembly of God in 1997, Lindell Cooley was leading worship. The service had broken into such a blissful sweet sustained time of corporate worship that he was moved to say a statement which has become a major part of my life

Chapter Six: The Gospel of Communion Part 2

and perfectly describes this stage of resigning to His presence. He said, "I don't want to offend God's Spirit by just rushing on." To the degree that you only want Him, you will find such comfort and rest in the nothingness of simply looking at Him, just enjoying His nearness. As Dr. Robert Gladstone once describe this as, "enjoying the covenant." Here is where many issues of the heart are settled.

To this day, I keep a notebook next to me when I sit with Him, to write down anything that He shows or speaks to me about Himself. In the beginning, I weighed the significance of my communion with Him by how full the paper was at the end of my time. I eventually recognized that this is not the case; everything God does is enduring but not always understandable. Or should I say, it is always indelible but not always intelligible. Many times it could take weeks or even months to know what was actually happening to you as you stayed there in blissful adoration. We might leave without an intelligible speaking, but our hearts are soft and pliable from just enjoying contact with Him.

One time I was on a radio show that emphasizes signs and wonders. The host asked me about the most significant things that I had seen during extended times of seeking the Lord. I knew what kind of show it was and what they were actually pressing me to say, but my answer was essentially this: "I have seen incredible manifestations of all kinds, including visitations, visions, physical manifestations of gold dust, heavenly manna, oil, feathers, light flashes, sparks, and things such as supernatural deafness, being frozen in awe by the glory, tremors, shakings, surges of divine electric waves. But that thing which is most important to me is a love-sick, broken-hearted, pleasing pain in which my soul suffers out of satisfied longing for Him. This is where my heart becomes soft to obey the Lord. This is the most important thing to me, whatever way it comes about through His presence. This is all that matters — a heart that will obey God."

Once during my time with God, I was in this place of resignation, not looking to move on but just feeling the bliss of His person flow through my being. From this place of contentment, I entered into a vision: I was in a dark room and all I heard was a voice say, "Do you want to know what is coming?" I knew, like all of God's questions, that the obvious answer is not normally the right one, so I thought about it. I finally answered, "No Lord. I just want You, because I know that if I have You, no matter what the future holds, I will be just fine." This is what the resignation stage is all about, total contentment with God Himself. Above anything that He can do or will do — lead, instruct and manifest — we want His presence. Borrowing

Chapter Six: The Gospel of Communion Part 2

language from David, the man after God's own heart, one thing I ask for; one thing I seek after: to live my life in the sweetness of His presence so that I may continually behold Him, inevitably resulting in me becoming like Him (Psalm 27:4, 8; 17:15).

The sixth stage in the soul that experiences God's presence is what I call **INCLINATION**. This is a spiritual urge in a particular direction. Sometimes I call this the directive. These come in many ways, including visions, trances, instantaneous knowledge, overwhelming desires or leadings in the Scriptures or themes in the Scriptures. However it comes, it issues from His sweet presence and person. Everything issues from His presence because this is the atmosphere of God's working. Even from the beginning of time, we see the presence of the Spirit hovering over the void before He spoke to restore it (Genesis 1:2).

The reason why it is so important to place resignation before inclination is because God only breathes into the soul that is detached from other motives and things. The resigned heart is the foundation upon which God will build. He may not lead in this way every time, but not to worry; we are only there for Him and His wishes anyway. If God doesn't do it, we must be content to live without it. As He leads we follow. Communion with God is simply moving in concert with God through God into God to live unto God.

The seventh stage in the experience of God is **MEDITATION**. As God grants to us His words they must be unpacked, or as the Psalmist wrote, "The unfolding of your words gives light" (119:130). The definition of "fold" is concealing one part with another. That is exactly how God's voice is; one part conceals another. As we meditate upon God's directive He will unfold and reveal it to us. Meditation is holding His speaking in the light of His presence until it unfolds, revealing more light. Here is where God makes things intelligible, visible, communicable and "prayable". For in His light we see light (Psalm 36).

We must pray into the things God has shown us, especially the Scriptures He gives us. When we hold the Scriptures up to the light of God's presence in accordance with His directive, they suddenly come alive. When His sweet presence has opened my eyes to see the wonderful things in His Word, I feel as if the pages themselves are breathing. I love to read the Scriptures in His presence because I am addicted to the electric thrill of God's voice that comes through them. They are a like the straw through which the honey of heaven flows. In this vein, I liken meditation to the suction by which we receive that honey.

Chapter Six: The Gospel of Communion Part 2

Many times God gives men a reading pattern. What God has given me is a pattern to read one chapter from each of the Psalms, a Proverb, a gospel, a prophet, a letter and an Old Testament. I rarely ever get through the whole pattern, but I simply pick up where I left off. I am not in a rush because *haste always muffles our ears*. Everything is careful, deliberate and important, so I take my time and read the Scriptures differently from any other reading that I do. I am much more interested in "hearing" than "learning."

It is important to note that being able to hear God through the Scriptures follows an already established overview of the whole redemptive plan as revealed in the entirety of the Scriptures. All of us must have these basic parameters. It doesn't take that long to establish them, but they are crucial to protecting us against deception.

The eighth stage for experiencing God is **INTERCESSION**. Intercession is standing before God on behalf of men. Whenever God shares His heart with us, it will produce in us inspired prayer. This is also directed by the Lord and wrapped in the sweetness of His manifested presence. He will share His sorrow with those who will come close enough to hear His heartbeat. Leonard Ravenhill once said, "I would rather pray than be the greatest preacher in all the world." Intercession is the surest sign of intimacy with God for as a man draws near to God's heart he will hear and feel what lies inside. Union with God is the merging of ecstasy and agony; the ecstasy of His presence and the agony of His heart. We pray out the things God has revealed in us.

The ninth stage is **REVELATION.** This is the unveiling of Jesus who is so infinitely glorious that no part of His glory is ever repeated; He is like a constant waterfall of new life and new vision. Even what we think to be "old" is brand new in His presence because He makes all things new. In His presence, nothing can grow old or stale, dry or dead. As He leads us into meditation, intercession or a mix of both, we will find an unveiling of His person that is fresh and original. I have found while praying into the things God has specifically shown me that they expand far more than they did by meditation alone. I have also seen that as I intercede in concert with the Spirit, suddenly the inspiration in prayer unveils more of God's heart and intention.

Revelation is the means by which God transfers His substance into us. It is also the means by which we can transfer the glory we have seen to others. It is the means by which God will direct our praying in accordance with His divine plan. There is no substitute for the revelation of Jesus for it shows us God's perfect Son and will in motion.

The tenth stage in the soul that experiences God is **IMPARTATION.** God literally dispenses Himself into us through revelation. This is so important: *God makes us like His Son by revealing His Son which imparts His Son to us.* The revelation of God is how we receive an impartation of God.

This impartation leads to the **TRANSFORMATION** of the inner man. Jesus Himself was transfigured through communion with God in God's presence, so our place of transformation will be no different. Such a transformation will cause an effortless **DEMONSTRATION** of God's own life through our lives. A life that is animated by daily transformative experiences of God is a life being interwoven with His, that is to say, being renewed day by day, and being conformed into the image of God's dear Son. There is no greater witness in this life than a God-filled man.

In conclusion, I submit to you that the means of such a demonstration is a divine transformation through an impartation that comes through a revelation of Jesus that will only come through the wonderful inclinations that happen in the resignation to His presence that we find in adoration, which is the beginning, the sustaining and the end of our experiential union with God.

Chapter SEVEN
THE GOSPEL OF JESUS

"It matters not how much we know of methods or doctrines or power. What really matters is the knowledge of the Son of God. Knowing God's Son is the way, knowing God's Son is the truth, and knowing God's Son is the life. Our power comes from knowing His Son. All that God gives to us is His Son, not a lot of things. Hence the whole question lies in knowing God's Son."

-Watchman Nee
Christ the Sum of all Spiritual Things

Chapter Seven: The Gospel of Jesus

"I am the way the truth and the Life…"
-John 14:6

If I said, "Jesus is our salvation," I don't know of any professing Christian that would offer a rebuttal; as a matter of fact, most would nod their heads in complete agreement without fully understanding what this statement actually means. Salvation is generally understood as being saved from sin and eternal damnation through accepting Jesus' sacrificial/substitutionary death on the cross. Such an understanding, though correct, still falls miserably short of what that salvation actually means. "Jesus is our salvation," means that we have been saved from all the repercussions and the hell of a life without Jesus. Let me explain further.

Jesus said, "I am the way," because He knew, you and me. He knew that our propensity is to seek to find a way to serve Him and forget about Him. He knows that we as humans adopt religious devotion, morality and good works as Christianity. He knows that we try to change our habits and live according to new, positive principles, claiming life through His saving power. But Christianity is not a *change* of life but an *exchange* of life. Christianity is life for life.

For the most part, most of us Christians have settled for a new belief system of morals connected with faith in God through Christ. We live in keeping with our new moral code and stamp Christ's name upon it, speaking our new religious language and steering clear of forbidden things, expecting the world to look at us and see Jesus. For too many of us, we make our own decisions and direct our own lives with our do's and don'ts, happy that we no longer live like the rest of the world who do not know or live by our new-found truths. Dear reader, I fear that we have lost Jesus as the *way*, where He literally directs us in His ways and leads us in His paths.

"Jesus is the way" means that we have been saved from a life that is lived apart from the *instruction of His presence and voice.* Have you ever considered that Salvation means we have been saved from the worthless path that He never intended us to travel? Do you understand that our own way, living out of sync with God, is an evil thing? (Isaiah 53:6)

It is very important to take this revelation to heart, because *it is an evil thing to get out of step with God* no matter how logical, productive and wise our own way seems. There is a way that seems right to a man, but the end thereof is death. (Proverbs 14:12) Man's ways always lead to death no matter how right they appear. Peter thought and spoke from a natural, human perspective and Jesus called Him Satan (Matthew 16:22). The mind of man is natural, earthly

Chapter Seven: The Gospel of Jesus

and demonic (James 3:15). We need to regularly look to the Lord, humbly surrender our way, and trust Him to lead us as our literal Good Shepherd. Jesus must be our way. Isn't it funny that Jesus saw Peter's plans as getting in front of Him (Matthew 16:23).

Jesus said, "I am the…truth" because He knows that men will cling to truths but forget Him who is the Truth. History shows us that the human way is to separate God from our practice unto Him. We have a great blessing in the written Word, through which He has given us certain truths as guidelines for life in this world. But He never intended for us to learn them and practice them without His empowerment; He never intended for them to replace His presence. Rather, He wants to breathe and speak His very self into us through the things written.

I can't tell you how many times during street evangelism that I've come across that partier who knows more Scripture than me or that homeless man who can quote the whole book of Galatians. These men only learned truths but they do not know Him who is the Truth. They only have a mental image of Christianity; they neither hear Christ nor see Him because there has been no life exchange.

Jesus said the same to the Pharisees who staunchly advocated the words of God with all their might and yet were unable to see the Word of God right in front of their faces. Jesus said to them, "You have neither heard His words nor seen His form." Jesus teaches us through this that *the Spirit of religion is devotion to God without a living perception of Him.* Jesus was devoted to God through perceiving interaction with Him.

Pilot asked Jesus the question, "What is truth?" I believe Jesus was completely silent before Him because if Pilot couldn't see the living Truth standing before him, no amount of lesser truths could help Him. We have lost Jesus as the *Truth* and have replaced Him with *truths*. Because of this, men have judged their spirituality and nearness to God upon their knowledge of the Bible.

Dear friends, the Bible is only the means to bring us into a position of hearing His voice so that we may know Him. The words written must be written in us and only His presence can perform such a wonder. It is true that God will not speak contrary to the Scriptures but it is equally true that He speaks to us through the Scriptures in order for us to know Him who is the Truth.

Jesus said, "I am the…life," because He knows that everything, no matter how religious or Spiritual, is absolutely lifeless without His presence. He knows that men seek to live their lives for Him without drawing life from Him. I know that every single one of my failures was first the failure to let Christ be my life. This is the heart of the spirit of religion: "Give them everything but His presence." Why? Because only His presence gives life. This is why some hate religion and why others die under it, because it only gives a picture of Jesus but never introduces the person of Jesus. Without the presence of Him who is life there is only death.

Jesus laid down His life so that He might be our life; He gave His life to give life to those of us who give Him our lives, not just theologically, but in reality. Jesus is not just righteousness *for* us, He is righteousness *through* us. Many might deny this, but this is the way of the Spirit: being animated by Christ Himself. He actually must be our quickening life, our state of being.

We have been saved from the life that we received from our natural fathers. After the fall, Adam reproduced after his own kind. Everyone lives from a defiled life source, defiled blood bent against God, towards self-preservation. Jesus came to rescue us from this selfish life by giving us His own life that is united with God's. As Leonard Ravenhill said, *"Jesus didn't come to make bad men good, but to make dead men live."* Our doom is that without the life of Christ, we do not posses life in ourselves. "He who has the Son has life and He who has not the Son has not life" (1 John 5:12). Jesus is the Life, our divine animation, the righteous quickening of our being.

So if you have been looking for the Way, look no further, for you can find it in Jesus, His presence and person. If you have been looking for the Truth, look no further for it is Jesus, His presence and voice. If you are tired and worn out, lifeless and powerless, receive supernatural influence and strength from Jesus, for His presence and Word is the Life.

In conclusion, there are two questions in the eighth chapter of the book of John that the Pharisees ask Jesus that I believe expose the very heart of the spirit of religion. They asked Him, "Where is your Father?" and "Who are you?" Herein, I believe, lies the heart of the attack of the spirit of religion that is dominating people's lives, even in Christianity.

The question, "Where is your Father?" indicates a lack of awareness of God's presence, "Where…is…your Father?" The first issue with the religious is there is no perception of God's presence in their lives. The first attack of the spirit of religion on a believer is to cause them to have no real connection with God's presence. It is as if the enemy is saying, "keep everything going, practices, language, songs, schedule, devotions, just don't let them experience God's presence."

The second question "Who are you?" follows a lack of God's presence simply because it is the means by which Jesus is revealed. The religious person has no real revelation of the person of Jesus. The heart of the attacks on the Christian life is a revelation of Jesus. The unveiling of the Son is everything. True Christianity is a revelation of Jesus. If the enemy can block your vision of Jesus you will remain blind and unable to walk with God. For any true walk with God is an endless vision of Jesus. In conclusion, it is important to note that the spirit of religion has these man areas of attack, "Where is your Father?" and "Who are you?"

APPENDIX
DRAW NEAR

Appendix: Draw Near

> *"Do not be as the horse or as the mule which have no understanding, whose trappings include bit and bridle to hold them in check, otherwise they will not come near to you."*
> *–Psalm 32:9*

This scripture describes the decision we must make about how we will live our own lives. This is not a suggestion but a direct warning from God against living without revelation. For our own protection, He has said with clear and firm voice, "Do not be…" Life without the revelation of Jesus Christ, no matter how successful, will reduce you to the life quality of a beast who lives according to its own passions, those whose God is their stomach and whose cravings are their guides (Philippians 3:19). God says to not live like a horse or a mule that has no revelation or understanding.

The wayward man must have trappings (external laws or life situations) to hold him in check because his passions and inward rebellion cause him to abandon the Master. This is true for every one of us who lives without revelation; without our revelatory link with God, we are led by our passions. Most, if not all of us, have gone through seasons of life where God placed us into situations to cause us to cling to Him more intensely in order that we would learn to lean on Him. Though these times are extremely painful, these times actually prove His mercy and grace to us.

Our passions can only be tamed by experiencing the unveiling of His holy person. Without revelation, our passions and animalistic nature take control. This is rebellion against God and an extremely dangerous way to live. God must continually put uncomfortable things into our lives to cause us to return to Him, not because He wants to torture us, but because we must be trained to recognize our need for God or we will be destroyed.

Too often, we foolishly wander away from His presence, thinking that we can live on our own, but eventually find ourselves picking up the pieces of our broken lives, wishing we had stayed near to the Lord. It is far more costly to disobey God than it is to obey Him.

The psalm specifically states that the bit and bridle will keep the horse in check, otherwise the horse *will not come near*. Nearness to Jesus is the issue; His presence is the issue. Even without too much introspection, you know who you are and I know who I am. Without His empowering presence, we are deeply in need of God every single moment. Remember the bit and bridle are for us. They pull us away from the death of our rebellion. If we draw near to the Lord and stay near Him, remaining dependent upon Him, the bit and bridle will no longer be needed.

If a man wishes to be absolutely worthless to the Lord and destructive to himself then all he must do is not take time to draw near and listen to the Lord and then stubbornly do whatever he wants to do. We must understand that distance from the Lord means idolatry. Idolatry is to cease to be utterly dependent upon His presence trusting in something, anything else.

Dear reader, say with my heart, "I desperately desire you and need your presence to deliver me from the destruction of what I am apart from you." Friends, in all honesty, if I am not immersed into His presence by yielded adoration, I am edgy, antsy, nervous, foolish, lustful, discontent, competitive, depressed, etc. We must trust in Him or we will forfeit the light of His presence. I am constantly recognizing over and over that the quality of my life is a mirror of the quality of my fellowship with God.

I want to make this very clear for each of us who desire to walk with God: we must draw near to God and live in His presence—listening to His voice, receiving revelation and spiritual understanding, remaining in the heart of God's protective guidance.

Otherwise, God in His mercy will use whatever means possible to teach us to depend upon Him. Choose to draw near to Him and He promises to draw near to you (James 4:8).

SPIRITUAL MAXIMS

Spiritual Maxims

I would rather speak one statement from heaven in the course of my whole life, than write libraries of intellectual brilliance.

To say, "Everyone has the Life of God already in them, they just need to wake up to it," is like saying, "I slept through an electrocution."

My soul can not be fully comforted, nor perfectly refreshed, but in God only, who is the embracer of the meek and lowly in heart.
–Kempis

"Jesus understands the source and arrival of 'life' to be connected to the timing of belief..."
-Dr. Jeff Hubing on John 5:24

Some see themselves as a need to God, others a purpose; but we are His desire.

Everyone says, "God you are all that I want." But their lack of joy, peace, contentment and satisfaction testify against their profession.

Give all for all. Keep nothing of your own love. The love of self hurts you more than any other thing in this world.
-Thomas A. KEMPIS

The phrase, "My Father..." will always be a stumbling block for the religious.
-See John 5.16-18

Many times our greatest need is a revelation of the things that we "already know."

The presence of the Spirit enjoyed in our daily lives is the both the evidence of and benefit of the resurrected Christ.

I believe it is important not to take your office into your closet.

When love and surrender mix in your soul, God Himself has become your strength.
-See Psalm 18.1

The strength to die with Him comes from a life of dining with Him.

Our senses are constantly ambushed by our surroundings, but the presence of Jesus frees us from their influence. This is called REST.
There is a constant frustration of desire that brews in the soul but the presence of Jesus literally frees us from it. This is called
REST.

Spiritual Maxims

There is a constant stress that the tick of time puts upon the soul but the presence of Jesus literally frees us from it. This is called REST.

The person of the Spirit means that communion in God's empowering presence is now our source of life, joy, peace, instruction and direction.

Christ's open invitation to come into His presence will overtake our lives and cause all other desires and interests to vanish.

Some say, "We cannot live by experience." It sounds "safe" but don't fall for it. Without experience we don't live.

Spiritual competition means that our heart is divided.

The focal point of an open heaven and angelic activity is the presence of the Son of Man.
-see John 1.51

The majesty of the Lord is manifested when He exercises His dominion in the earth through men.
-see Psalm 8

Effort is when we apply our soul to the particular act itself while walking in the Spirit is lifting our soul to God and He becomes the act.

Pride: It is the custodian of all sin. Every failure was first the failure of self exaltation.

Pride: It will, little by little, whether you can perceive it or not, erode you and your life from the inside out. (Proverbs 16.18)

Pride: God hates it-no matter who you are, how gifted you are, how long you've followed Him or how grand your achievements. (Proverbs 16.5)

Stillness is the antithesis of rebellion.

When worship flows out of the soul joy flows into the life.
-See Luke 1:46

To be in love with Him means loving to be with Him.

"It is good that one should wait quietly for... The Lord."
- Lamentations 3:26

Those taken by deception can trace their blindness back to a point where His presence was no longer their source of instruction.

Those being choked by religion can trace that hold back to a point where they let truths replace the person of Christ.

Spiritual Maxims

Every one of my sins can be traced back to my failure to allow Christ to be my life.

Our works are simply the light produced from the internal combustion that occurs when God mixes His presence with the human soul.

Yielding to the Spirit means the complete venerable offering of your soul to be possessed entirely by God and absolute trust in Him alone.

I know how quickly a person can forfeit the joy of the gospel.
-Martin Luther

"My agenda makes Him close His mouth."
-Madonna Awad

Jesus said, "I am the way" because He knew that man, by nature, would walk upon principles, rather than the direct guidance of His voice.
Jesus said, "I am the truth" because He knew that man, by nature, would cling to truths surrounding Him and forget all about Him.
Jesus said, "I am the Life..." because He knew that man, by nature, would find a way to live for Him without drawing life directly from Him.

Some of us are waiting for something to happen when we are in His presence, not recognizing that His presence is the happening.

Many people's spiritual senses are numbed in the closet by all the pressure they put on themselves to be in there and accomplish something.

Sometimes the Lord will sit completely still for a while, just to see if our personal ambition will move us on without Him.

It is very simple. Man, by nature, is self centered. That is why he gravitates toward doctrines that magnify him.

When do you have 'first love' for Jesus? When He alone captivates you and only His presence fills you with overwhelming joy.
–Schlink

"Retain the standard of sound words...which are in Jesus."
- Paul's advice to Timothy

Our business is the announcement and administration of Christ's all-conquering Kingdom, until He returns to exercise full dominion over all.

Spiritual Maxims

Fight against all internal resistance to absolute trust in God.

"If anyone...does not agree with sound words, those of the Lord Jesus Christ...he is conceited and understands nothing."
-1 Timothy 6.3-4

The satisfaction of the soul is not some "perk" of His presence, but rather the means by which He empowers and frees us to obey Him.

God goes before those who keep Him before them.
-Thinking of Psalm 121

If we go ahead, we are not led.

"...He called you through our gospel, that you may gain the glory of our Lord Jesus Christ."
- 2 Thessalonians 2:14

How does one protect God's voice in their life?
Simple OBEDIENCE.

David is not in denial about his troubles, he is simply preoccupied with the wonder of God's voice in his life. See Psalm 119:161

Even a brother in the Lord can become a friction against you if he has something before the Word of the Lord in his heart.

The Kingdom is inside the Son, not the other way around.

"Jesus Christ died for us so that we will live together with Him."
-see 1 Thessalonians 5:10

The sweet bliss of His presence in sustained adoration, settles my mind, inspires my will, satisfies my longings and makes Him all my desire.

What does it profit a man to reason high secret mysteries of the Trinity, if he lacks meekness, whereby he displeases the Trinity?
–Kempis

Anything outside of that which comes from waiting on the Lord is a lesser operation.
– Brian Guerin

I have no personal position to preserve. If God has made me His prophet, then let Him show it.
-T. Austin Sparks on Moses

Spiritual Maxims

Without the Word of the Lord coming into our hearts, affliction will drain all the life out of us.
-See Psalm 119.107

"...in simplicity of heart seek Him."
-The Book of Wisdom 1:1

Revelation does not come from years but rather the sweet honey that drips from His lips in His presence.

In haste there is much waste.

His Will is in His Words.

Abandonment to God is manifested in seeking out His voice.

Daily enjoyment of the life of the Living Word is how we live by and experience our Salvation.

Journal Entry March 2001: "Prayer is a place of rest and refreshing. Relax. Focus. Wait and follow His leading."

As gospel preachers we are restorers of the Divine Order.

There is no accomplishment so grand to exempt a man from the judgment seat of Christ.

It is the presence of the Spirit that reveals the present Christ whispering to our hearts through the Scriptures.

Becoming still is only the beginning. Sustained stillness is real Spirituality.

Man was, is and will always be more comfortable with doing than with yielding, simply because it makes more sense to him.

The answer is not found in the realm of zeal...rather it is...an absolute original and new apprehension of Christ.
–T. Austin Sparks

The prophets words are windows to the world to come.

The world today is well-nigh bankrupt of real prophetic ministry, in this sense - a voice that interprets the mind of God to people.
–T. Austin Sparks

It is true that the gospel never comes in word only, but it is also true that it never comes without words.

Spiritual Maxims

Those who have personal interests in view are entirely out of keeping with the objective of God's kingdom and glory.
-Harry Foster

Never under any circumstances will He accept those who refuse to trust Him.
-Harry Foster

In His presence you are free from the need to have anything else and your soul seems to be frozen in a state of the delight.

Once the Spirit enters the soul it is awakened to sensations far superior to that to which it was previously bound knowing only the physical

To bring up a family in a godly home is a service to God, all too much in danger of being forgotten in our popular ideas of God's service.
–Harry Foster

God is looking for those who will share with His King the responsibility for the glory of His kingdom.
-T. AUSTIN SPARKS

If your heart is lifted up, even your wisdom and knowledge delude you.
- see Isaiah 47.10

We hear because He is here.

The final judgment will be based on the degree of glory found in our lives. Nothing else will be of lasting importance.
-T. Austin Sparks

Contrary to natural reason, the dominion of the Son is brought into being as He rests in His Father's presence.
–see Psalm 110

Jesus prayed - and still prays - that we may also persevere in prayer.
-Harry Foster

We can drift out of the will of God but we can never drift into it.
- Harry Foster

Only that way which comes from the Lord is worthy of the Lord.

To not wait on the Lord is to have already eclipsed Him in your heart.

Only the revelation of stewardship can bring me out of my closet.

The fact that Jesus is a person is the irrefutable evidence that experience is the only way to know Him.

We must stop saying, "I've failed; I cannot come to God." We must start saying, "I've failed; I must come to God."

When God revives a heart, a life of prayer begins.

When we really walk in the stillness of His presence, we recognize how demonic stress really is.

In the midst of thousands of HEARTS burning with fervent passion, God looks for one that is SOFT enough to listen to and OBEY His VOICE.

A soft heart is God's greatest treasure.

One of the most common ways that the devil blinds Christians to the power of the gospel is by some new "revelation."

No amount of accumulated degrees will raise your spiritual temperature.

The proud man is damaged by that which he would have been delivered from had he acknowledged his need for God.

Did you know that the origin of all our sins is not to be animated by God's Spirit?

The Word they heard did not profit them because they refused to relinquish their lives to it.
-Hebrews 4:2

The natural man is addicted to activity and lives by movement, therefore the sweet still nothingness of God will always be nonsense to Him.

In the lives of modern Christians, nothing is as important, nothing is as simple, and yet nothing is so neglected as fixed adoration of God.

The greatest "golden calf" sculptors in the world are those who simply will not wait on the Lord. Idols are mostly fashioned by impatience.

I will go on to visions and revelations of the Lord.
– Paul

It is in waiting on the Lord that the soul's receptivity is open.
Backsliding in heart is no longer being satisfied with God alone but satisfying yourself.
-See Proverbs 14:14

Spiritual Maxims

When we enthrone anything in our hearts other than God, God retires and lets the other god do what it can.
-O. Chambers

So often it is our devotion to our agenda that robs us of the divine mingling that occurs through waiting in the bliss of His presence.

Every corrected church in Revelation had one core issue: a need for a fresh revelation of Jesus.
–David Popovici

How blessed is he who strives after Thee alone.
- Henry Suso

As long as you want to protect your image of your spirituality, you will find yourself in conflict with the operation of His Life.
–Art Katz

"Your eyes will behold your Teacher. Your ears will hear..." Isaiah 30

Save us from cliché, easy, cheap phrases that are hollow and give us the real inward knowledge of Yourself.
-Art Katz

Enjoying The Gospel

Come God and breathe a deeper sense of Thyself into our souls.
-Art Katz

Only those who can't see Him have a hard time adoring Him.

In waiting on the Lord there is no "until" — waiting is the inward disposition of subjectivity that brings out the Divine Life.

To take refuge in the Lord means to rest your whole mind, will, and affections in loving trust and submission to God's presence alone.

The greatness of a man isn't found in the shining of his platform but the radiance of his closet.

Adam's curse was having to live life before God without life from God.
-Ark Katz

The only way to live for God is by God.
-Art Katz

There is no such thing as a consistent abiding in Christ apart from a consistent renunciation of self.

Oars are forbidden in the river of God.

Spiritual Maxims

90 percent of prayers vanish in His presence.

When our lives are an investment in the age to come, the difficulties of this life lose their potency.

Trials in this life sting in exact proportion to our investment in this life.

Adoration is like air in the Kingdom of God.

Never let what your eyes see trump what God has previously shown you.
-Brian Guerin

Some people get alone with God and never actually touch Him simply because they do everything but worship.

We abide in the Lord by enjoying constant fellowship with Him.

We are never more humble than when we adore Him.
-Andrew Murray

The cost of not having listened to God is far more than the cost of listening to Him.

The spirit of seduction promises delight without commitment.
- Journal entry, spring 2008

No voice no peace.
–Michael Dow

"What I have heard from the Lord... I make known to you." -Isaiah 21:10 (the prophet speaks into your ear what God has spoken into his ear)

Jesus is not just righteousness for us but righteousness through us.

We constantly have to deny ourselves in order for the Christ life to emerge.
-Fulton Sheen

If we are not conscious of Him, how could we ever walk with Him?

"People say they want to know God but they are unwilling to take the time to develop a relationship with Him."
-Steve Hill

Spiritual Maxims

Christ teaches us that true prayer recognizes the establishment of the kingdom of God as the chief purpose of the divine will.
-A.B. Simpson

If you come to Him, He will ALWAYS receive you.

Is there a clearer way to say "the becoming is in the looking," than, "they that look to Him are radiant"?

May we never find a platform until we have found a grave.
–Michael Dow

Don't cover the flame in your heart to comfort the ice in another's.

"Whoever listens to Me will live...and be at ease." - Proverbs 1:33

We receive His Life for fellowship and then we fellowship to receive His Life.

If you will not receive His words you have no right to speak His words.

Only those who stand before God on behalf of men will stand before men on behalf of God.

Godliness is the exhale of having inhaled God.

Adoration is our link to The Internal Divine Nature.

God has installed in us the means by which we can receive the empowering communicative impulses of Himself.

God's man is made in the closet.
-E.M. Bounds

Some people are of such a weak constitution that they feel that they would die if they entered silent prayer.
-St.Teresa of Avila

Every false theology is a failure to recognize that God is exactly like Jesus Christ.
-Gordon Fee

"When one walks love-sick for God, he is at the heights of prayer life...fulfilling the greatest commandment to perfection."
-Thomas Dubay

"Wisdom is in the presence of God."
-Proverbs 8:30

God Himself has taught us how to pray, "Go into your closet, shut the door..." Silence and solitude are God's idea.

The Water is flowing at all times.
-St Teresa of Avila

If God's purpose for giving Himself to you was ministry then He would not call you as His bride but as His surrogate.

"When the eyes of the soul looking out meet the eyes of God looking in, heaven has begun right here on this earth."
-A.W. Tozer

"Genuine worship involves feeling."
-A.W. Tozer

This is for certain: EVERYONE who does not wait on the Lord will come to poverty. -See Proverbs 21:5

Only the enjoyment of Christ can keep us in right relationship with God.
–Lee

The best prayer is not that we speak to the Lord but that the Lord speaks to us.
–Lee

"My eyes shed streams of water because men do not obey You."
-David, Psalm 119:136

"...adore Him...behold His beauty and inhale Him. To pray is to spiritually breathe the spiritual air, which is the Lord Himself."
-Lee

Most people cannot ascend into God in prayer because they are latched onto weights of motives other than his presence.

We are called to produce signs of God's new world within the apparently unpromising landscape of the old one.
-N.T. Wright

Embrace the pain and rejection of being forgotten, ignored or not taken seriously, knowing that it is an invitation to Union with God.

To the degree that we value being in sync with God we will hate everything out of sync with God.

The true cause of all human trouble is that mankind is out of the divine order.
-A. B. Simpson

The real remedy for all that needs prayer is the restoration of the kingdom of God.
-A. B. Simpson

Dear reader, when was the last time you wept at the Master's feet?

ABOUT THE AUTHOR

Eric William Gilmour is the founder of Sonship International based in Orlando, Florida. He is an itinerant prophetic teacher and the author of several books, *Union--The Thirsting Soul Satisfied In God, Burn--Melting Into The Image of Jesus, Into the Cloud – Becoming God's Spokesman*, and a co-authored book with Michael Dow, founder of the Burning Ones International, and David Popovici, founder of Kingdom Gospel Mission, entitled *Divine Life; Spiritual Conversations*.

God spoke to Eric in 1998 calling him to give his life to preach the gospel throughout the world as His spokesman. In 2010, Eric began Sonship International and has since traveled throughout the world, preaching the gospel and witnessing the power of the Holy Spirit working miracles, signs and wonders.

Above all, Eric is burdened to see the church come into a deeper experience of God in their daily lives. He founded Sonship International for this very purpose, to inspire the sons of God to delight in the presence and voice of God and become a voice to this generation.

Also from Eric W. Gilmour

Into The Cloud

The prophet has become his message. He does not prepare messages, he speaks what has been spoken into him; he speaks what has been spoken into him; he speaks what he himself has become." "Obedience is when a man's life is yielded to the extent that God can perform through that man the things He has spoken to him." "We must seek to find Christ present in the depths of the scriptures, not merely as type and shadow, but as the living word, the present speaking of God."

ISBN: 978-1-59755-367-4

$14.99

NOTES

NOTES

NOTES

NOTES

NOTES